NAIL ART DESIGNS

A BEGINNERS GUIDE TO BASIC

NAIL ART DESIGNS

Jacqueline Neal

NAIL ART DESIGNS

A BEGINNERS GUIDE TO BASIC NAIL ART DESIGNS

Jacqueline Neal

NAIL ART DESIGNS

**A Beginners Guide to Basic
Nail Art Designs**

Credits

Publisher: Jacqueline Neal
Editors: Elaine Clark and Marina Lucky

Photographs: Jacqueline Neal
             Marine Lucky

Cover Design: Jacqueline Neal
Cover Photos: Jacqueline Neal

© 2011 Jacqueline Neal

For information:
Dawkins Publishing Company
P. O. Box 386
860 Dan River Road
Spartanburg, SC 29330

Neal, Jacqueline
        Nail Art Designs/ Jacqueline Neal

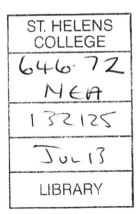

Special Thanks:

Thanks to Marina Lucky
Elaine Clark and Catherine Powell

Thank to my
husband for his support and patience.

Authors Notes:

I hope this book will assist you, the reader
in overcoming the many challenges
nail art designs can bring.

Jacqueline Neal

CONTENTS

FOREWORD

This is not just any nail art book. What you have in your hands is a book developed to help you, the reader improves your nail art skills.
When it comes to getting results, the principle lesson I've learned is to be patience and practice. Your results will depend on how often you practice and how much patience you have. If you are fully committed to becoming a great nail artist, the sky is the limit. Remember the keys to success in nail art designs are **patience, practice and perseverance.**

NAIL ART DESIGN is a step- by- step guide to nail art designing. This book provides various nail design ideas for the beginner nail artist and anyone with an interest in nail art. To derived the most benefit from this book, and to become successful in nail art designing, the aspiring nail artist should practice each technique as often as you can. It is the author's hope that this book will provide quick answers and information in developing your skill in nail art designing.

ABOUT THE AUTHOR

Jacqueline Neal began her successful career as a licensed nail technician 15 years ago in Las Vegas, Nevada. She has worked in numerous nails and hair salons from Las Vegas to South Carolina. She enjoys nail art designing and believes that there are others who share her passion, as well. In the course of her career, she realized that there are many challenges in nail art designing. In 2005, she started developing and designing this book to help overcome some of these many, many challenges.

Jacqueline Neal is a graduate of Marinello Schools of Beauty, where she received her training for a nail technician. She became a licensed nail technician shortly thereafter. She attended the University of Phoenix where she received a Bachelors' of Science in Business Administration and a Masters in Management. She is pursuing a Bachelors of Arts in English, with a concentration in writing from Converse College.

Jacqueline and her husband lives in South Carolina where she owns, operates and manages "The Pedicure Queen Nail Services," a company that specializes in nail care and nail art designs. For advice or questions about nail art or this book, feel free to email her at:
jacqueline.neal61@yahoo.com

ACKNOWLEDGEMENTS

I wish to acknowledge the many individuals who encouraged me to write NAIL ART DESIGNS. Their input enabled me to produce this book which will be of value to everyone with an interest in nail art designing. To all those who contributed, I extend my sincere thanks and appreciation: Zelotes Dawkins, Anna Hood, Kasey Neal, Michelle Neal, Jeree Weaver, Cherelle Beard, Charnell Robinson, Charnice Beard, Michael Robinson, Ronald Robinson, Jada Jackson, Chris Jackson, Demaron and Jay.

Special thanks to Marina Lucky for her beautiful photographs. Elaine Clark for her endless hours of editing, and Catherine Powell for her legal advice. I sincerely thank each of you. I know you are equally as proud as I am for your contributions and guidance supplied in the development of this book.

INTRODUCTION

To those of you that love decorating nails but are not quite sure where to start, this book will take you on a journey giving you step-by-step guidance in developing and designing nail art.

NAIL ART DESIGNS is a comprehensive book written from a professional point of view that shows nail designs ideas in a quick and easy to read format. You will discover not only how to do simple nail designs, but also what specific tools, techniques and materials to use.

Most of the products mentioned in this book are available through beauty supply, craft, and discount stores.

NAIL ART DESIGNS offers endless opportunities in developing and expressing your individual creativity.

NAIL ART DESIGNS turns nails into canvases where you can display your individual personality and provides many ideas on creating artistic nails designs.

There are numerous websites that offer instructions on nail art designing, but there is nothing more convenient as having this step-by-step nail art designs book right at your finger tips.

The secrets to creating beautiful nail art designs are **patience, practice** and **perseverance**. Chose a design, follow the instructions, and watch how your nail art skills improve and develops

GETTING STARTED

Before starting any design, you must have the tools and supplies needed for each design. The beginner nail designer may not have or can not afford expensive equipment. No need to worry. Various tools can be use to make beautiful designs on natural or artificial nails. For example, a toothpick or water-based felt tip can be used to make dots or lines. Sponges can be use to make abstract designs. Nail tape, confetti, glitter, appliqués (nail art stickers), artificial flowers, rhinestones and nail charms are just a few more, and can be found at any beauty supply store, craft store or discount store. Many manufactures' offer nail art pens in numerous colors for nail designs as well. So a beginner nail artist has many tools and supplies to choose from.

Acrylic paint is recommended for use in making designs because this paint is washable when mistakes are made. So any mistakes can be removed with ease. If using nail polish, be sure to work quickly before the polish dries.

Wherever you find your tools and supplies and whatever tools and supplies you use, remember that you are not limited to what is mention in this book.

MAKING BASIC SHAPES

Dots, circles, lines, triangles are some of the basic shapes used in nail art designing.

DOTS
A small nail art brush, a dotter or a toothpick are some of the tools that can be used to make various sizes of dots. Simple dip one of the tools in acrylic paint or nail polish to make the desired size.

CIRCLES
Dip a nail art brush, dotter or a toothpick in acrylic paint or nail polish and make a dot. Swirl the dot until you reach the desired size.

LINES
Use a fan brush, a stripping brush, or a toothpick to make various sizes and width of lines.

STARS
Make any size dot. Then drag points from the dot to create a star.

HEARTS
Make a dot on one side of the nail; drag to a point. Make another dot on the other side, drag it down so that the two points meet.

FLOWERS PETALS, TEARDROPS, LEAVES
Make a dot, use a toothpick to drag the dot to a point.

Remember to be patience and practice, practice, practice.

Freehand painting involves using tools such as, stripping brush, fan brush and yes, even toothpicks for each design. You can use one or two tools to make an artistic design.

Tools Needed
Nail polish
Basecoat
Topcoat
Any nail art brush
Toothpick (if desired)

Procedure
Polish nails the desired color.
Let dry. If you are not sure what color complements your base color, locate the color wheel in the back of this book. After choosing your complementary color; choose the nail art tool you want to use. Using your chosen tool, draw straight or wavy lines. In the designs below, we have used a stripping brush to make lines, and a toothpick for making small dots.
Let dry. Finish with top coat

1   FREEHAND PAINTING

One of the simplest ways to add creativity is to add glitter or confetti. Glitter and confetti adds a bit of shimmer and sparkle to nails. Nails look glamorous for any special occasion.

Tools Needed
Glitter or Confetti
Nail glue or clear polish
Basecoat
Topcoat

Procedure
Apply desired color. To catch excess glitter or confetti, use a piece of paper. Apply glue/clear polish on the area you want to cover with glitter or confetti.
Sprinkle the glitter or confetti over the area.
Tap finger to eliminate excess glitter.
Cover with two layers of clear polish to seal and let dry.

Gems and rhinestones are available in many types, shapes, sizes and are easy to apply. They make nails sparkle and shine.

Tools Needed
Nail polish
Basecoat
Topcoat
Orangewood stick or tweezers
Gems or Rhinestones
Glue

Procedure
Polish nails in desired color.
Apply the glue in the area you want to apply gems or rhinestones, designed. Apply gems or rhinestones. Let dry.
Apply top coat. Do not apply to quickly or air bubbles can appear.
Let dry. Finish with top coat.

Foils are fantastic and easy to use. Create amazing, stunning and unique nail art designs with nail art transfer foil.

Tools Need
Transfer foil
Adhesive or glue
Basecoat (if desired)
Topcoat

Procedure
Polish nail in desired color.
Cut foil to desired size.
Press foil design side up onto nail. Rub onto the nail until the backing paper lifts.
Pell off the backing.
Seal with topcoat. Let dry.

Abstract designs give diversity to each nail. With abstract design, each nail will be like an individual canvas. If you want something bold, try abstract designs.

Tools Needed
Nail polish
Basecoat
Topcoat

Procedure
Using two or more complementary colors of polish or acrylic paint, (in the designs below black is used as the desired color and glitter polish for abstract effect.) Make irregular line, dots or circles
Let dry. Finish with top coat.

Marbelling is a type of nail art that looks like swirls, but is done with water. Although marbleizing can be some what messy, each design will be amazing and different.

Tools Needed
Any size container
Two or more colors of nail polish.
Basecoat
Top Coat

Procedure
Apply base coat. Let dry. Using room temperature water, drop 1 color of nail polish into the water. Allow it to spread. Before the polish dries add 2 drops of another color on top of the first color. Using a toothpick, cuticle stick or swirling tool, drag the colors into desired design. Dip nail into the design. Let dry. Finish with top coat and let dry.

Swirl designs are easy to do and give each nail a unique appearance. Imagination is the key to these designs. Jewells, decals, rhinestones, charms or dangles can be added for enhancement.

Tools Needed
Nail polish
Basecoat
Topcoat
Any swirling tool

Procedure
Polish nail with desired color
Before polish dries, add one or two complementary colors. (We have use two) Swirl into desired design
Let Dry.
Finish with top coat.

7 SWIRL DESIGNS

Sponge designs are very simple and easy to make. Each design will be unique, different and can be done in less than thirty minutes.

Tools Needed
Nail polish
Basecoat
Topcoat
Any type of sponge

Procedure
Polish nail desired color.
Before polish dries, dip sponge into desired polish or paint to make desired design.
Let Dry.
Finish with top coat.

French designs have been a favorite of women since its introduction in the early eighty's. Although done with traditional white polish, French designs can be done in other colors as well. French designs can be done diagonal, horizontal or sideways on the nail.

Tools Needed
Base coat
Any color nail polish
Top coat

Procedure
Polish nail with base coat
Using your desired color, polish nail in a diagonal, horizontal design
Let dry. Finish with top coat.

Appliqué's, stickers and pre- design tips make beautiful and unique nail designs. These various nail art supplies are available in beauty supply stores, craft stores and discount stores.

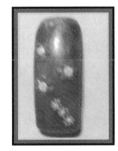

Real lace gives nails a soft sensuous look and creates unique designs on nails. Whether you use real lace or create the impression of lace, the outcome will be gorgeous.

Tools Needed
Lace
Brush on nail glue or adhesive
Nail polish or basecoat
Top Coat

Procedure
Apply nail polish or basecoat. Let dry.
Cut lace to desired pattern.
Starting at the cuticle area, brush on glue.
Apply lace onto the nail.
Using a toothpick, press down on the lace to secure it to the nail.
Add another coat of glue and press down again.
Let set for about a minute, then trim excess lace using a nail clipper or a nail file.
To smooth the lace, buff slightly with the soft side of a nail file.
Finish with top coat.

11 LACE NAIL DESIGNS

Holidays designs are a great way to celebrate the holidays. The designs below are only a few you can offer your client. Use your imagination.

Fourth of July
Halloween
Christmas
New Years

NAIL ART GALLERY

NAIL ART GALLERY

NAIL ART GALLERY

NAIL ART GALLERY

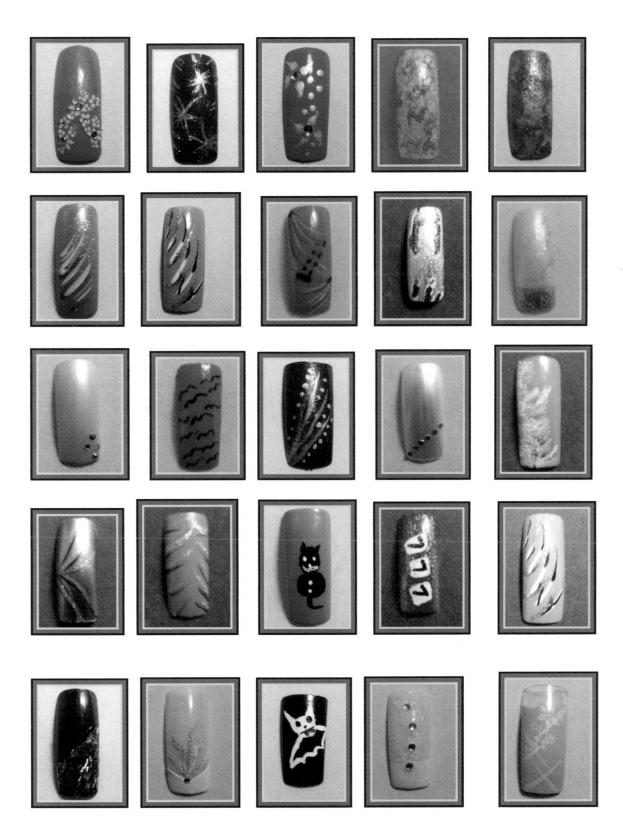

NAIL ART GALLERY

NAIL ART DESIGNS

A Beginners guide to basic nail art designs

In this book, you will find:

Everything you need to created beautiful designs
Photographic instructions
No artistic genius required
Over 100 Nail Art Designs Ideas
How-to- step by step instructions

CPSIA information can be obtained
at www.ICGtesting.com
Printed in the USA
LVIW021526130613
338479LV00006B

* 9 7 8 1 4 6 8 0 7 7 2 6 1 *